PRAYERS TO GROW BY

Contents

This book and how to use it 7

In the Morning 8
Our Homes 10
Your Beautiful World 12
Forgive Us, God 14
Animals and Pets 16
Help Us to Please You, God 18
For Sad Days 20
All the Countries of the World 22
God Cares 25
For Happy Days 26
Our Families 28
When We Feel Frightened 30
Please Teach Us, God 32
Our Friends 34
Helping and Caring 36
Summer Holidays and Vacation 38
When We Are Ill 40
Coming and Going 42
Hot Days and Cold Days 44
Time for Play 46
For the Light 48
Loving and Giving 50
Busy Days 52
Please Help 54
We Praise You, God 57
For Our School 58
Wet Days and Windy Days 60
Thank You, God 62
People at Work 64
Your Word, the Bible 66
At Night Time 68

Special Prayers
for Special Times 71

Christmas 72
Easter 74
Whitsun/Pentecost 76
Harvest and Thanksgiving 78
Sunday 80
Birthdays 82
Graces 84
Prayers for God's Blessing 86
Prayers of Jesus 88

Subject Index 90
Index of First Phrases 91
Acknowledgements 93

This book and how to use it

All the prayers in this book have been specially chosen for children's use, at home, in school and at church. The actual words, as well as the ideas, of most of them are within a child's understanding and experience. But we have also included some of the great Christian prayers of other ages, because they are part of our spiritual heritage. Although somewhat removed from everyday speech, they convey their own sense of worship and of the greatness of God. Each double page is complete, bringing together a number of prayers, old and new, simple and more complex, on a particular subject which will appeal to children and relate to their own lives and experience.

The photographs and drawings are an integral part of the book, intended to delight even the very young child who cannot read the prayers. Prayer time should be a natural and enjoyable part of our whole relationship with God, an essential part of life as God intended it to be, a key element in the new life in Christ. The themes have been chosen to give variety and are rooted in everyday living, in familiar joys and fears.

The book lends itself to family use, day by day at breakfast or bedtime, or Sunday by Sunday, by parents and children together. It is also an invaluable source book for teachers at school and in church. The list of contents and supplementary subject index will help in choosing topics or particular prayers for specific occasions.

Making this book has been a real pleasure. Our hope is that it will give equal pleasure and help to all who use it.

In the Morning

God's mercies are new every morning.
From Lamentations 3

I can say it to my family, I can say it to my friends,
I can say it at school—so I'll say it to you—
Good morning, God, you're Great!

May my mouth praise the love of God this morning.
O God, may I do your will this day.
May my ears hear the words of God and obey them.
O God, may I do your will this day.
May my feet follow the footsteps of God this day.
O God, may I do your will this day.

Prayer from Japan

Dear Lord Jesus, we shall have this day only
once; before it is gone, help us to do all the
good we can, so that today is not a wasted day.

From a prayer by Stephen Grellet (1773-1855)

Father, we thank you for the night,
And for the pleasant morning light;
For rest and food and loving care,
And all that makes the day so fair.
Help us to do the things we should,
To be to others kind and good;
In all we do at work or play
To grow more loving every day.

Now another day is breaking,
Sleep was sweet and so is waking,
Dear Lord, I promised you last night
Never again to sulk or fight.
Such vows are easier to keep
When a child is sound asleep.
Today, O Lord, for your dear sake,
I'll try to keep them when awake.

Ogden Nash

Thank you, God, for the day-time when I can be awake
and busy. Thank you for all there is for me to do today:
new things to find out, friends and games to play with.
Thank you for the sun that gives us warmth
and light to see by.

Our Homes

Jesus went in to stay with them.
From Luke 24

God of all our cities,
Each alley, street, and square,
Pray look down on every house
And bless the people there.

Lord Jesus, we are glad that you lived in a happy home. Thank you for our fathers and mothers, and for the way they love and care for us. May we love and help them.

Please God, look after all those who stay behind at home when others go out to school, or work or play. Bless the ones who are too young or too old to go, and those who look after them. Bless those who get things ready for us when we get home, and help us to say thank you to them.
We pray especially for those who stay at home because they are ill.

May the love of God our Father
Be in all our homes today:
May the love of the Lord Jesus
Keep our hearts and minds always:
May his loving Holy Spirit
Guide and bless the ones I love,
Father, mother, brothers, sisters,
Keep them safely in his love.

Visit, we beseech thee, O Lord, our homes and drive far from them all the snares of the enemy: let thy holy angels dwell therein to preserve us in peace; and may thy blessing be upon us evermore; through Jesus Christ our Lord.

Office of Compline

Your Beautiful World

And God saw everything that he had made,
and it was very good.
From Genesis 1

God, this is your world,
you made us, you love us;
teach us how to live in the world that you have made.

Loving Father, we praise you for the wonderful things
which you have given to us:
For the beautiful sun,
For the rain which makes things grow,
For the woods and the fields,
For the sea and the sky,
For the flowers and the birds
And for all your gifts to us.
Everything around us rejoices.
Make us also to rejoice and give us thankful hearts.

Heavenly Father, thank you for the beauty and wonder
of your great creation.

It's your world, God.
From the top of my favourite tree
There are lots of things to see,
Children are playing on the grass,
Mums with clothes pegs in their mouths,
Babies crying,
Nappies drying,
Grandpas smoking, soaking up the sun,
Watching this year's carrots come.
It's your world, God;
I like it.

Forgive Us, God

Forgive us the wrongs that we have done,
as we forgive the wrongs that others have done us.
From The Lord's Prayer, Matthew 6

Our Father in heaven:
Please forgive me for the wrongs I have done:
For bad temper and angry words;
For being greedy and wanting the best for myself;
For making other people unhappy:
Forgive me, heavenly Father.

O God, you made us and you love us, thank you for being so willing to forgive us. Make us quick to own up to you whenever we do wrong so that we may quickly be forgiven. Then our day will not be spoilt by worry and we can be happy all day long, through Jesus Christ our Lord.

Lord Jesus Christ, we confess to you now
the wrong things we have done,
the wrong things we have said,
the wrong in our hearts: please forgive us
and help us to live as you want us to.

Lord Jesus, we remember how you forgave the people
who hurt you. Help us to forgive those who hurt us.
May we never try to pay them back.

Forgive me, Lord, for thy dear Son
The ill that I this day have done.
That with the world, myself, and thee,
I, ere I sleep, at peace may be.

Bishop Thomas Ken (1637-1711)

Animals and Pets

Lord, you have made so many things!
How wisely you made them all!
The earth is filled with your creatures.
From Psalm 104

All things bright and beautiful,
All creatures great and small,
All things wise and wonderful
The Lord God made them all.

He gave us eyes to see them,
And lips that we might tell,
How great is God Almighty,
Who has made all things well.

Our Father, thank you for our pets – for friendly cats
and dogs and rabbits. Help us to take great care of them.

Thank you for the beasts so tall
Thank you for the creatures small.
Thank you for all things that live
Thank you, God, for all you give.

Dear Lord Jesus, our little dog has died. We cried
because she was so loving and good. She made everyone
happy. We are glad it's you who've got her now.
Please take care of her, but of course you will.
You love all animals. You made them all.
Thank you for letting us have her first
and for all the happy times we've had with her.

Father we thank you for animals that help us, for cows
sheep and horses; dogs that guard us and those that guide
the blind. We thank you too for all rare and strange
animals and for those that make us laugh.
May we take good care of them all.

Dear Father, hear and bless
Thy beasts and singing birds;
And guard with tenderness
Small things that have no words.

Help Us to Please You, God

Happy are those who obey God with all their heart.
From Psalm 119

Lord, through this day,
In work and play,
Please bless each thing I do.
May I be honest, loving, kind,
Obedient unto you.

Help us to keep the promises we make to you,
O God.

Open my eyes that I may see,
Incline my heart that I may desire,
Order my steps that I may follow
The way of thy commandments.

Lancelot Andrewes (1555-1626)

Dear Lord Jesus, please help us to do what our parents
and teachers tell us, even though we may not want to.
We know that we shall be obeying you, and showing that
we love you, by doing straightaway as we are told.

Lord, on the way to goodness, when we stumble, hold us,
when we fall, lift us up, when we are hard pressed by
evil, deliver us, when we turn from what is good, turn
us back, and bring us at last to your glory.

Day by day, dear Lord, of thee
three things I pray:
to see thee more clearly,
love thee more dearly,
follow thee more nearly,
day by day.

Richard of Chichester (about 1197-1253)

19

For Sad Days

In times of trouble God will . . . keep me safe.
From Psalm 27

L ord Jesus, I pray for those
who will be unhappy today:
for mothers who have no food
to cook for their children;
for fathers who cannot earn
enough money for their families;
for children who are sick
or frightened;
and for those who are alone
and without people to love them.

D ear Lord Jesus, you cried when your friend Lazarus died,
so you understand how we are feeling today. Comfort us
as we are sad and lonely without the one we loved so much.
Help us to be glad that our friend is happy with you
and free for ever from sadness and pain. Teach us to trust
and love you so that we too may live with you for ever.

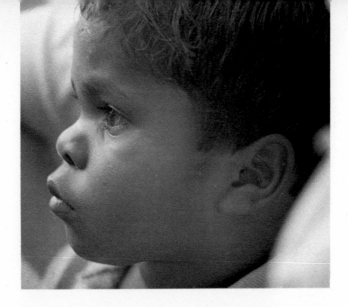

Comfort, O Lord, we beseech thee, all who mourn for the loss of those dear to them. Be with them in all their sorrow, give them faith to look beyond the troubles of the present time, and to know that neither life nor death can separate us from the love of God which is in Christ Jesus our Lord.

Lord Jesus, you know that we are sad today. Help us to cheer up, because you love us always and are close to us all the time.

The Lord is my shepherd;
I have everything I need.
He lets me rest in fields of green grass
and leads me to quiet pools of fresh water.
He gives me new strength.

He guides me in the right way,
as he has promised.
Even if that way goes through deepest darkness,
I will not be afraid, Lord,
because you are with me!
Your shepherd's rod and staff keep me safe.

From Psalm 23

All the Countries of the World

God loved the world so much that he gave his only Son,
so that everyone who believes in him may not die but
have eternal life.
From John 3

Space counts for nothing, Lord, with thee;
Thy love enfolds each family
Across the ocean, far away,
And here at home where now we pray,
And praise thee for thy care this day.

Please guide the leaders of many different countries
at the meetings where they try, by working together,
to make the world a better and a safer place. Help them
to want peace rather than power, and show them how they
can share the food in the world so that no one need be
hungry.

Dear Father of the world family,
please take care of all children everywhere.
Keep them safe from danger,
and help them grow up strong and good.

O Lord, help us who roam about. Help us who have been placed in Africa and have no dwelling-place of our own. Give us back our dwelling-place. O God, all power is yours in heaven and earth.

Prayer of an African chief

God our Father, Creator of the world, please help us to love one another. Make nations friendly with other nations; make all of us love one another like brothers. Help us to do our part to bring peace in the world and happiness to all men.

Prayer from Japan

God Cares

Look at the birds flying around: they do not plant seeds,
gather a harvest and put it in barns; your Father in heaven
takes care of them! Aren't you worth much more than birds?
From Matthew 6

God who made the grass,
The flower, the fruit, the tree,
The day and night to pass,
Careth for me.

When I wake up in the morning,
thank you, God, for being there.
When I come to school each day,
thank you, God, for being there.
When I am playing with my friends,
thank you, God, for being there.
And when I go to bed at night,
thank you, God, for being there.

I bind unto myself today
The power of God to hold and lead,
His eye to watch, his might to stay,
His ear to hearken to my need;
The wisdom of my God to teach,
His hand to guide, his shield to ward;
The word of God to give me speech,
His heavenly host to be my guard.

St Patrick (389-461)

Lord, how glad we are that we don't hold you
but that you hold us.

Prayer from Haiti

For Happy Days

Sing for joy to the Lord, all the world!
From Psalm 100

Praise God, from whom all blessings flow;
Praise him, all creatures here below;
Praise him above, ye heavenly host;
Praise Father, Son and Holy Ghost.

Bishop Thomas Ken (1637-1711)

My heart is overflowing with praise of my Lord,
my soul is full of joy in God my Saviour.
The one who can do all things has done great things
for me – oh, holy is his name!

From The Magnificat (Luke 1)

Let us with a gladsome mind
Praise the Lord for he is kind;
For his mercies shall endure,
Ever faithful, ever sure.

All things living he doth feed,
His full hand supplies their need:
For his mercies shall endure,
Ever faithful, ever sure.

John Milton (1608-1674)

Thank you for each happy day,
  For fun, for friends,
and work and play;
Thank you for your loving care,
Here at home and everywhere.

O Father of goodness,
  We thank you each one
For happiness, healthiness,
Friendship and fun,
For good things we think of
And good things we do,
And all that is beautiful,
Loving and true.

Prayer from France

Dear Father of us all, we thank you for all
  the happiness of every day. We thank you for all
the good things you give to us.
Help us to make other people happy too.

Thank you, God, for this new day
  In my school to work and play.
Please be with me all day long,
In every story, game and song.
May all the happy things we do
Make you, our Father, happy too.

O God, look on us and be always with us that we may
  live happily.

Prayer of the Amazulu people

Our Families

God gives families to the lonely.
From Psalm 68

God bless all those that I love;
God bless all those that love me:
God bless all those that love those that I love
And all those that love those that love me.

From an old New England sampler

We thank you, God, that everyone who loves you belongs to your family. You are our Father, we are your children. Thank you, God, for the worldwide family of your people. Thank you for our brothers and sisters the whole world over.

Thank you, Lord, for grannies and grandads. Thank you for the stories they tell us and the things they help us make. Thank you that they have time to tie up our shoes and take us for walks. Please bless them all.

Dear Father, please take special care of children whose mother or father has left home. Help them to know that you love them, that you are always near to comfort and keep them safe.

O God, the Father of all families, make our family like the family where Jesus grew up, and our home like his home, where we all care for each other and share our things with each other, so that there is enough for everyone. Show us what to do when we feel jealous, or want our own way, or don't want to help.

God bless all the aunties
Who are kind to girls and boys;
God bless all the uncles
Who remember birthday toys.

Bless, O Lord Jesus, my parents and all who love me and take care of me. Make me loving to them, polite and obedient, helpful and kind.

When We Feel Frightened

When I am afraid, I put my trust in you.
From Psalm 56

Lord Jesus, I'm scared. Help me.
I needn't be afraid, because you are with me.
You are stronger than anything. You love me.
You will take care of me. Thank you.

All by myself with the door shut and the light out
I'm afraid. It gets so dark I can't see and the
noises seem so loud. The stories of witches and shootings
and news on TV get all mixed up and seem very real.
I'm scared so I need you, Lord.

Jesus, when I am afraid, help me to remember
that you are with me, nearer than my breathing,
closer than my beating heart. You understand my fears
better than I do, so let me trust in you and give me the
grace to support others in their fears as you support me.

When I know how much you love me, Jesus,
and that you're always with me,
I can talk to you about being afraid.
You understand. You won't laugh at me.
Give me courage, make me brave,
not just tonight – but tomorrow as well.

The King of love my Shepherd is,
Whose goodness faileth never;
I nothing lack if I am his
And he is mine for ever.

Henry Williams Baker (1821-1877)

O God, who knowest us to be set in the midst of so many and great dangers, that by reason of the frailty of our nature we cannot always stand upright; grant to us such strength and protection, as may support us in all dangers, and carry us through all temptations; through Jesus Christ our Lord.

Book of Common Prayer

Please Teach Us, God

Teach me your ways, Lord,
make them known to me.
Teach me to live according to your truth.
From Psalm 25

O Lord, open my eyes,
to see what is beautiful;
My mind, to know what is true:
My heart, to love what is good:
for Jesus' sake.

T each us, good Lord, to serve thee as thou deservest;
To give and not to count the cost;
To fight and not to heed the wounds;
To toil and not to seek for rest;
To labour and not to ask for any reward
Save that of knowing that we do thy will.

Ignatius Loyola (1491-1556)

W hen I pray I speak to God, when I listen God speaks
to me. I am now in his presence. He is very near to me.

L ord Jesus, take me this day and use me.
Take my lips and speak through them.
Take my mind and think through it.
Take my will and act through it,
and fill my heart with love for you.

O God, make us children of quietness
and heirs of peace.

First-century prayer by St Clement

God be in my head, and in my understanding:
God be in mine eyes, and in my looking:
God be in my mouth and in my speaking;
God be in my heart, and in my thinking;
God be at my end, and at my departing.

From The Book of Hours (1514)

O make my heart so still, so still,
When I am deep in prayer,
That I might hear the white mist-wreaths
Losing themselves in air!

Utsonomiya San – Prayer from Japan

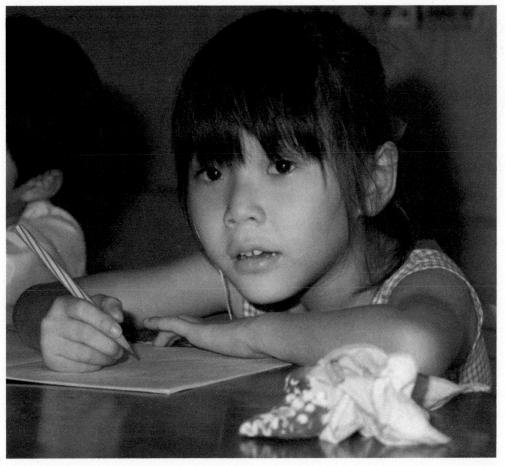

Our Friends

A friend loves at all times.
From Proverbs 17

Jesus, friend of little children,
Be a friend to me;
Take my hand and ever keep me
Close to thee.

Dear Lord Jesus, I am thankful for my true friends,
but I would have you for my dearest friend.
Let me love all my friends, but love you most of all.
Make me, like you, a friend of all children.

Lord Jesus, you want us all to live together
as friends, sharing our differences
and giving our help. Please teach us to be loving,
patient with the people who are slower than us,
and friendly with those who are shy.

Thank you, God, for friends.
Thank you for fun and games and parties.
Thank you for my best friend.
Help me to be a good friend and keep my promises.
Help me to be friends even with those I
don't much like – because you love us all.

Jesus, when you were on earth you had friends
who were especially close to you. You knew what it was
like to enjoy their company; you also knew what it was like
when they deserted you. Please keep my friends
in your care. Help me to be a good friend.

We thank you, loving God, that when we come to say
sorry, you are always ready to forgive. Please help
us to be like you. When people say sorry to us
may we forgive them straightaway, ready at once to be
friends again.

Helping and Caring

Help carry one another's burdens.
From Galatians 6

Thank you, O God our helper, for all who help you to
look after us. For mothers and fathers, and all who
look after us in our homes. For teachers who help us
at school, and for all who teach us what you are like.

Lord, make me an instrument of thy peace;
Where there is hatred, let me sow love;
Where there is injury, pardon;
Where there is discord, union;
Where there is doubt, faith;
Where there is despair, hope;
Where there is darkness, light;
Where there is sadness, joy.

St Francis of Assisi (1182-1226)

Lord Jesus, show us something to do for you:
something loving to say, something kind to do,
somebody to comfort, something lovely to make.
Help us to watch with your eyes for chances to
do your work because we love you.

Thank you, God, for all good people; for people
who are strong and brave when others are afraid;
for people who help others to be happy and good;
for people who are cheerful when things go wrong.
Thank you, God, for all good people.

Two little eyes to look to God;
Two little ears to hear his word;
Two little feet to walk in his ways;
Two little lips to sing his praise;
Two little hands to do his will
And one little heart to love him still.

Summer Holidays and Vacation

The whole earth is full of God's glory.
From Isaiah 6

Dear God, thank you for our holidays:
for the sunshine, the fresh air,
the lovely open spaces and the sea.
Thank you for this chance to see other places
and to meet different people.

Thank you, God, our heavenly Father, for holiday joys
beside the sea. For pebbles and rocks and shells and sand;
for the blue sea and for the fun of playing in the water.

We thank you, God, that you will be with us today as
we go on our outing. Please give us a happy time.
Keep us safe and help us to discover new and interesting
things.

Praise to God for summer days,
For summer clothes and summer plays,
And for our summer holidays.

Lord Jesus, be with those who have no happy holidays, who have never seen the sea or played in the fields. If there is something we can do to make them happier please show us, and if there is something we can share, help us to do it gladly for your sake.

Thank you, God, for holidays
In the lovely summer days,
For our picnics, for our fun,
For our playing in the sun.
Make us good, with smiling faces,
So our homes are friendly places,
And the helpful things we do
Make all our mothers happy too.

When We Are Ill

The Lord will help him when he is sick
and restore him to health.
From Psalm 41

Lord Jesus, I am ill.
Please make me well.
Help me to be brave,
and thankful to the people
looking after me.
Thank you for being here with me.

You're marvellous, God, loving everyone the way you do.
I don't like having to stay in bed but when I talk to
you I know you love me and that's great. Some children
always have to stay in and never get out to make friends.
Love them too, and help them. Loving everyone is difficult.
I can't do it but you can manage it, God. Perhaps I'd
better try and learn. Teach me now while I'm ill and
there's plenty of time.

Lord Jesus, who for our sakes became a man, and who showed your love of children by taking them up in your arms and blessing them: we ask you to bless those who are ill. Your love for them is greater than ours can ever be; therefore we trust them to your care and keeping.

Great Father in heaven, thank you for doctors and nurses everywhere. Thank you for giving them clever brains to know how to make us well, and gentle hands to bandage cuts and sores.

Tend thy sick ones, O Lord Christ, rest thy weary ones. Bless thy dying ones. Soothe thy suffering ones. Pity thine afflicted ones. Shield thy joyous ones. And all for thy love's sake.

St Augustine (354-430)

Coming and Going

The Lord will protect you as you come and go.
From Psalm 121

Thank you, God, for the fun of travelling. Thank you for jets and helicopters, liners and yachts, for rockets and spacecraft, underground trains and escalators; for cars and trains, scooters and lorries. Please watch over all who travel today. Give them commonsense and politeness. Teach them to guard against accidents and to obey the rules made for their safety.

Loving heavenly Father, who takes care of us all,
please bless all the people on the roads today:
please bless the people driving buses, cars and lorries,
please bless the people riding bicycles and scooters,
please bless the people walking and crossing busy roads,
please help them to be careful on the roads today
and help us to be careful when we cross the roads.

Alone with none but thee, my God,
I journey on my way.
What need I fear, when thou art near,
O King of night and day?
More safe am I within thy hand
Than if a host did round me stand.

St Columba (521-597)

God of all the steamships sailing far away,
God of all the railways running every day,
God of all the travellers on bus or car or plane,
Guard and guide them every one and bring them home again.

Bless all those I shall meet today, and help us to
help each other.

Hot Days and Cold Days

While the earth remains, cold and heat, summer and
winter shall not cease.
From Genesis 8

O ye summer and winter, bless ye the Lord,
Praise him and magnify him for ever.

Benedicite

H eavenly Father, thank you for the joys of winter:
for snow and wind, and sparkling frost;
for cosy fires and indoor games;
for warm clothes, and the shelter of our homes
on stormy nights; thank you, heavenly Father.

D ear God, who made the world, we thank you for the
winter. We thank you for the cold, frosty days,
when we jump and run and keep warm; for snow and
the fun we have with it; for warm clothes and good
fires and hot dinners.

W ind and ice and shrouding snow
At thy bidding come and go;
Clouds obscure or planets shine,
But they serve thee and are thine.

W e thank you for the beautiful snow,
for the warmth it gives to the earth,
and for its quietness.
Help us to be quiet enough
to hear your voice speaking to us
and to obey it always.

44

Dear Father God, who made the world, we thank you
for the summer. We thank you for the warm sunny
days, for our summer clothes, for the games we play
out of doors and all the nice things that summer brings.

We thank you, O loving Father,
for the joys that summer brings;
for warm days and soft breezes,
for the trees and the flowers.
Help us to remember
that all lovely things come from you.

Time for Play

For everything its season and for every activity its time.
From Ecclesiastes 3

Dear God, thank you for our toys –
big ones and little ones,
old and new ones,
the ones we play with,
the ones we take to bed with us.
Help us to share our toys
with other children and to say 'thank you'
to the people who gave them to us.

Dear God, thank you for books:
big serious ones, thin funny ones,
books with pictures
and books that tell stories;
and thank you for the people who write them.

Give me, Lord, each day, time to pray,
time to serve and love, time to work and create,
time to do nothing and time to be still.

L oving Father, on this day
Make us happy in our play,
Kind and helpful, playing fair,
Letting others have a share.

D ear God, we enjoy watching programmes on television,
especially those which are exciting and interesting.
Thank you for all the people who make the programmes –
the performers and producers,
the cameramen and engineers,
and those who write the stories and play the music.

O ur Father, maker of this wonderful world,
thank you for Saturday, for holiday time
and freedom and the open air.
Come into all I am going to do today
at home, out of doors, with my friends.
Help me to enjoy everything
you have made for me. For Jesus' sake.

T hank you, God, for the gift of music.
May I not neglect it, but use its power and beauty
to lead me nearer to yourself. Whether I sing or play
or listen, and whether the music is a hymn or a song
or a symphony, may I be blessed through this gift of yours,
and cherish it always.

For the Light

God is light and in him is no darkness at all.
From 1 John 1

May the Lord Jesus Christ, who is the splendour
of the Eternal Light, chase far away all darkness
from our hearts, now and for evermore.

Praise him, sun and moon,
praise him all you shining stars!

From Psalm 148

O thou great Chief, light a candle within my heart
that I may see what is therein and sweep the rubbish
from thy dwelling place.

Prayer of an African girl

O God, who hast folded back the mantle of the night
to clothe us in the golden glory of the day,
chase from our hearts all gloomy thoughts
and make us glad with the brightness of hope.

Ancient Collect

Thank you God for my eyes.
Thank you for the beauty of the world.
Thank you for all that my sight does for me.
Please support those who have no sight.
Please help me to remember the needs of the blind.
Please help me to remember that blind people
are ordinary people who cannot see.
Thank you God for my eyes.

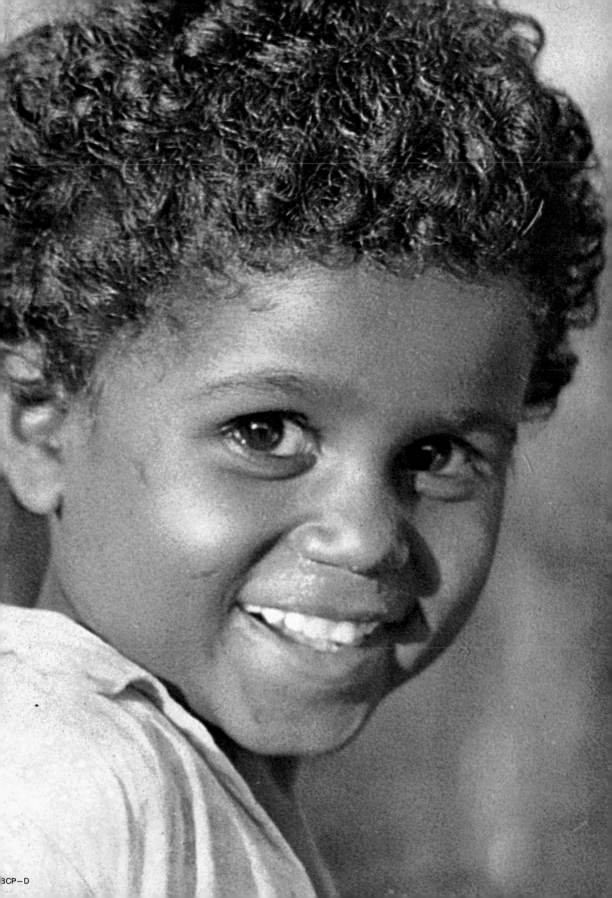

Loving and Giving

We love because God first loved us.
From 1 John 4

Love and praise to you we give
By whose love all creatures live.

Father in heaven, we praise you that so many people
love us. Thank you most of all for your own great
and wonderful love. Make us loving too.
Grant that we may show our love by helping other people,
for the sake of Jesus.

Put love into our hearts, Lord Jesus –
love for you; love for those around us;
love for all we find it hard to like.

O Lord, help us to put you first; others next;
and ourselves last, now and always.

Help us, Lord, to be thankful
for the gifts we have received from you
and to share with others who are in need.

Lord of the loving heart, may mine be loving too,
Lord of the gentle hands, may mine be gentle too.
Lord of the willing feet, may mine be willing too,
So may I grow more like to thee
In all I say or do.

Eternal God, the light of the minds that know thee,
the joy of the hearts that love thee,
the strength of the wills that serve thee;
Grant us so to know thee that we may truly love thee,
so to love thee that we may fully serve thee,
whom to serve is perfect freedom.

Gelasian Sacramentary

Busy Days

Work, for I am with you, says the Lord.
From Haggai 2

Thank you for the joy that comes when we have done
a good piece of work, even if it means doing it over
and over again, as Jesus did in the carpenter's shop.
Thank you for the happy times we have when we do things
together, and share everything with each other.
Thank you for all our friends.

The things, good Lord, that we pray for,
give us grace to work for.

Sir Thomas More (1478-1535)

Dear Jesus, bless my hands today,
And may the things they do
Be kind and loving, strong and good,
Two busy hands for you.

Dear Lord Jesus, help us to enjoy the jobs we do
to help today: at home, when we clear away our toys
or wipe the dishes; at school, when we give out books
and tidy our classroom. May we do everything cheerfully
and well, because we love you.

Be my guide, O Lord, I pray,
Lest I stumble on my way.
Be my strength, dear Lord, I ask,
That I may fulfil each task.

Teach me, my God and King,
In all things thee to see,
And what I do in anything
To do it as for thee.

George Herbert (1539-1633)

Please Help

When Jesus saw this large crowd, his heart was filled with
pity for them.
From Mark 6

Dear Father God, we thank you that we are able to see
– please help the blind.
We thank you that we are able to hear
– please help the deaf.
We thank you that we are able to speak
– please help the dumb.
We thank you that we can run and jump and play
– please help sick and crippled children everywhere.

54

O God, who made the world
And all the people in it,
We pray for boys and girls
Who've never heard of you:
We pray that they may come to know
You are the loving Father
Of every girl and boy.

Heavenly Father, bless those who starve while we have
plenty to eat; those who are homeless while we lie
safely in bed; those who have no clothes while we throw
clothes away. Help us to care for those less fortunate
than ourselves and to do all we can to help them.

Dear Jesus, you were taken as a baby refugee
into Egypt, take care of all homeless wanderers,
of all who have to leave their comfortable homes
because of misfortune or war, and of all who have no homes
at all. Guide them with your love to find help and friends,
and to help each other in their loneliness.

Lord Jesus, we remember today the old people
living around us. Especially we think of those who are
lonely and poor and have no one to visit them
or take them out. Please help us not to forget them.
Thank you for all that they have done for us.
Help them to know that you are the Friend who never leaves
us or forgets us.

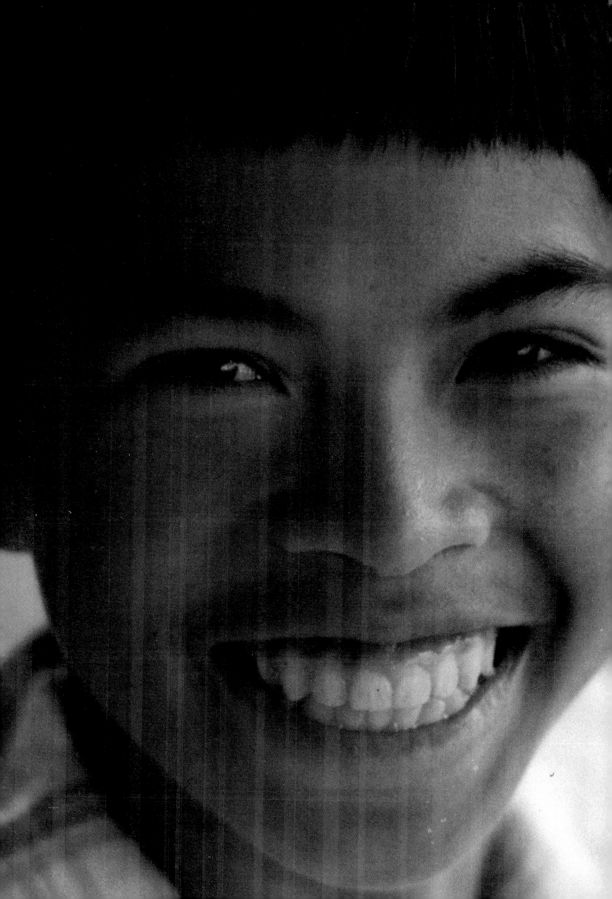

We Praise You, God

O come, let us worship and bow down, let us kneel
before the Lord, our Maker!
From Psalm 95

Dear God, you are so very wonderful: more wonderful
than the flowers, more wonderful than the sky,
more wonderful than the sun. We praise you: we bless you:
we worship you.

Holy God who madest me
And all things else to worship thee,
Keep me fit in mind and heart,
Body and soul, to take my part.
Fit to stand and fit to run,
Fit for sorrow, fit for fun,
Fit for work and fit for play,
Fit to face life day by day.
Holy God, who madest me,
Make me fit to worship thee.

Lord, thy glory fills the heaven,
Earth is with its fullness stored;
Unto thee be glory given,
Holy, holy, holy Lord.

Bishop R. Mant (1776-1848)

God, our loving Father, thank you that you never change.
You are as strong and wise and loving as the day you
made the world. Thank you that nothing can ever happen
that will make you alter. You are the one true God and
Maker of all. We worship you in Jesus' name.

For Our School

Whatever you do, work at it with all your heart.
From Colossians 3

O Lord, bless our school; that working together
and playing together, we may learn to serve you
and to serve one another.

O Lord Jesus, we remember how you had lessons to learn
when you were a boy. Help us to learn our lessons
well. Show us how to do our best, for your sake.

Father of all men, we pray for boys and girls of other
lands who go to our schools. Give them courage
as they live and work with those whose words and ways
are so different from their own, and help us to be
especially loving and friendly to them.

Father of us all, thank you for another happy day at
school. Thank you for the new lessons we have learnt
and the games we have played. May we come back tomorrow
ready for another happy day.

O God, our heavenly Father, we are so very glad of all the things we do in school: for the pictures we can paint, for the things we can make, for the books we can read, for the letters we can write, for the stories that we hear, for our music and our dancing, for the games that we can play, for our toys and for our friends. For all that we can do in school, for all our happy times in school, thank you, heavenly Father.

Thank you, God, for all our teachers
who come to school each day,
and for the teacher in our class
who helps us with our work.
Thank you, God, for all she does
to help us learn and understand:
thank you, God, for all she does
to help us grow up kind and good.
Bless her, God, and bless her work:
bless all the teachers in our school.

Wet Days and Windy Days

God provides rain for the earth, he sends the wind.
From Psalm 147

Our Father in heaven, we praise you for the gift of rain; thank you for giving rain to make the trees and flowers grow; thank you for sending rain so that we may have water to drink; thank you for the summer rain that cools the hot dry earth.

Thank you, God, for rain and cool water,
    which we need each day for washing and for bathing.
Help us not to grumble when a rainy day stops us
going out to play.

Thank you, heavenly Father,
    for the wind that dries and warms the earth
so that seeds may grow,
giving us food to eat and flowers to see and smell.
Thank you too for fun outdoors on windy days.

Thank God for rain
and the beautiful rainbow colours
and thank God for letting children
splash in the puddles.

A child's own prayer

Dear Lord Jesus, who did not fear the sea, guard all
fishermen and sea-going people. If danger comes,
help them to be calm and courageous and be with the people
who answer their call for help.

Dear God, be good to me, the sea is so wide
and my boat is so small.

Prayer of the Breton Fishermen

Praised be our Lord for the wind and the rain,
For clouds, for dew and the air;
For the rainbow set in the sky above
Most precious and kind and fair.
For all these things tell the love of our Lord,
The love that is everywhere.

Elizabeth Goudge

Thank You, God

Give thanks to the Lord, for he is good.
From Psalm 106

Thank you, God, for this sunny morning,
it makes me happy.

A child's own prayer

Holy God, I'm happy that I can bow in prayer before
you. Thank you very much. Thank you for the clothes
that we wear, and everything you give us, and for forgiving
us our sins. As you died on the cross for us,
be with us always.

Prayer of a Navajo Indian girl

For sausages, baked beans and crisps
For papers full of fish and chips
For ice cream full of chocolate bits
Thanks, God.
For furry caterpillars to keep
For woodlice with their tickly feet
For crabs we catch with bits of meat
Thanks, God.
For bicycles and roller skates
For playing football with my mates
For times when I can stay up late
Thanks, God.

Dear Father God, thank you for loving and caring for us
every day of our lives. Help us to remember your love,
and to love you in return.

Thank you for the world so sweet,
Thank you for the food we eat.
Thank you for the birds that sing,
Thank you, God, for everything.

People at Work

Do your work cheerfully, then, as though you served the Lord.
From Ephesians 6

Dear God, please look after everybody at work today: all those who drive buses and trains so that other people may go to work; those who work in mines and quarries to get material for others to use in factories and workshops; those who look after crops and animals on the farms to help with our food; those who catch fish for us to eat; those who bring our food to us and those who sell it in the shops. Bless all those who help to look after us.

O God, help us to remember the people working at night while we are asleep: for policemen walking in dark streets, and for the firemen watching for sudden fires; thank you, God. For engine drivers rushing their great trains through the night; thank you, God. For the men working in busy factories; thank you, God.

Please bless those who have no work, especially if they have had none for a long time. They must be very bored and unhappy. Please help their families to help them and give them some work to do soon.

God of the coalmine away under ground,
God of all workshops and wheels that go round,
God of all industry teach me to be
One of the many that labour for thee.

Dear God, we pray for the workers of the world.
For those who care for animals and those who grow our
food.
For those who mine the coal, and those who run the trains.
For those who buy and sell, and those who keep the house.
For those who tend the sick, and those who keep us well.
For those whose work is dangerous, and those whose work is
dull.
Dear God, we pray for the workers of the world.

65

Your Word, the Bible

Your word is a lamp to my feet
and a light to my path.
From Psalm 119

Father, we thank you for the Scriptures
which were written for our help and instruction.
Open our eyes to see the lessons that we can learn
from them.

Thank you, Lord, for those who gave their lives to give
us the Bible in our own language. Please help those
who are translating and printing the Bible in faraway places,
so that one day the Bible may be read in all the languages
of the world. Bless those who teach us to understand
what the Bible means, in our own country as well as in
other lands.

O God, please comfort all the people who want to read
the Bible but live in countries where they are not allowed to.
Please help them to remember any verses
they learned by heart a long time ago.

L ord, here is my Bible,
  Here is this quiet room,
here is this quiet time,
And here am I.
Open my eyes; open my mind;
open my heart; and speak.

B lessed Lord, who hast caused all holy Scriptures to be
  written for our learning; grant that we may in such wise
hear them, read, mark, learn, and inwardly digest them,
that by patience and comfort of thy holy Word
we may embrace and ever hold fast the blessed hope
of everlasting life, which thou hast given us in our Saviour,
Jesus Christ.

Book of Common Prayer

At Night Time

As soon as I lie down, I go quietly to sleep;
you alone, Lord, keep me perfectly safe.

From Psalm 4

Lord, keep us safe this night,
Secure from all our fears.
May angels guard us while we sleep,
Till morning light appears.

We thank thee, our heavenly Father,
through Jesus Christ, thy dear Son, that thou hast
graciously kept us this day; and we pray thee that thou
wouldst forgive us all our sins where we have done wrong,
and graciously keep us this night. For into thy hands
we commend ourselves, our bodies and souls, and all things.
Let thy holy angel be with us, that the wicked Foe
may have no power over us.

Martin Luther (1483-1546)

O God, my Guardian, stay always with me.
In the morning, in the evening,
by day, or by night, always be my helper.

Prayer from Poland

Good night! Good night!
Far flies the light;
But still God's love
Shall flame above,
Making all bright.
Good night! Good night!

Victor Hugo (1802-1885)

Now the busy day is done,
Father, bless us every one.
Keep us safely through the night,
Till we see the morning light.

Heavenly Father, as people turn to sleep,
please bless all those who cannot sleep tonight.
Comfort those who are sad.
Forgive those who have done wrong.
Calm those who are worried.
Help those who are in pain.
And grant your peace to every troubled heart.

Jesus, tender Shepherd, hear me;
Bless your little lamb tonight;
Through the darkness please be near me;
Keep me safe till morning light.

All this day your hand has led me,
And I thank you for your care;
You have warmed and clothed and fed me;
Listen to my evening prayer.

O Lord Jesus Christ, who received the children who came
to you, receive also from me, your child, this
evening prayer. Shelter me under the shadow of your wings,
that in peace I may lie down and sleep; and waken me
in due time, that I may glorify you, for you alone
are righteous and merciful.

Prayer used in the Eastern church

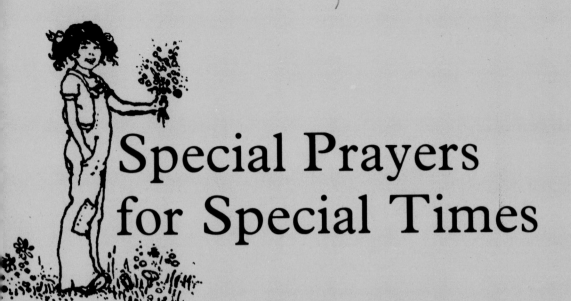

Special Prayers for Special Times

Christmas

Joyful news for everyone! The Saviour has been born.
From Luke 2

O Lord Jesus, who for love of us
lay as a baby in the manger,
we thank you that by your coming
you brought joy to all the world.
Help us at this glad time
to try to make others happy for your sake.

Thank you, God, for the joys of Christmas:
for the fun of opening Christmas stockings;
for Christmas trees with sparkling lights;
for exciting parties; for Christmas cakes and puddings;
thank you, God.
Thank you for all the happiness of Christmas-time;
thank you for all the lovely presents we receive;
thank you most of all that Jesus was born
as a baby on the first Christmas Day.
Thank you, God.

Grant, heavenly Father,
that as we keep the birthday of Jesus,
he may be born again in our hearts,
and that we may grow in the likeness
of the Son of God,
who for our sake was born Son of Man.

Jesus Christ, thou child so wise,
Bless mine hands and fill mine eyes,
And bring my soul to Paradise.

Hilaire Belloc

Dear baby Jesus, we have come to find you
in the stable at Bethlehem.
May we love you as Mary loved you.
May we serve you as Joseph served you.
May we worship you as the angels worshipped you,
Jesus, our King.

Easter

Jesus was given over to die because of our sins
and was raised to life to put us right with God.
From Romans 4

Good Friday is a time of sadness,
Easter is a time of gladness.
On Good Friday Jesus died,
But rose again at Eastertide.
All thanks and praise to God.

Jesus, you're alive!
Not as you were alive in Galilee with your friends.
  Then only the people who met you could talk to you –
but now, everybody can.

I'm talking to you and you're with me;
friends of yours all over the world
are talking to you now, this very minute,
and you're with them.

That's what I like about you –
alive for everyone.

Prayer from Holland

Jesus, who died for me,
Help me to live for thee.

Jesus, our Lord, we praise you
that nothing could keep you dead in the grave.
  You are stronger than death and the devil.
Help us to remember
that there is nothing to be afraid of,
because you are alive and by our side.

Whitsun/Pentecost

God has sent the Spirit of his Son into our hearts.
From Galatians 4

Holy Spirit, hear us,
Friend from heaven above.
Thou art ever near us;
Fill our hearts with love.

We thank you, heavenly Father,
that when Jesus went back to be with you in heaven
you sent us the Holy Spirit to take his place.
Though we cannot see him, we know he is at work
in the world in everything that is good and holy,
and in our lives to carry out your will.
Send us the Holy Spirit, we pray,
to shape and mould our lives and guide us day by day.

O God, we cannot do your will unless you help us.
Send the Holy Spirit into our hearts to show us
how to live.

Dear Holy Spirit, you are the one who comes along beside us to help and comfort us. Please make us sure that you are with us. You are the teacher who helps us to understand and remember what the Bible says. May we learn from you. You are God who comes to live in our hearts and love us. Help us to welcome you. For Jesus' sake.

O Lord our God, give us by thy Holy Spirit
a willing heart and a ready hand
to use all thy gifts to thy praise and glory;
through Jesus Christ our Lord.

Archbishop Cranmer (1489-1556)

O God, forasmuch as without thee we are not able
to please thee; mercifully grant that thy Holy Spirit
may in all things direct and rule our hearts;
through Jesus Christ our Lord.

Book of Common Prayer

Harvest and Thanksgiving

Every good gift and every perfect gift is from above,
and comes down from the Father.
From James 1

O thou who art Lord of the harvest,
The Giver who gladdens our days,
Our hearts are for ever repeating
Thanksgiving and honour and praise.

D ear God our Father, we thank you for all your care
for us; for our homes and food and clothes;
for our teachers and our friends;
and especially for our fathers and mothers.
Help us always to be thankful to you for all your great
goodness.

B lessed art thou, O Lord our God, King of the universe,
who bringest forth bread from the earth.

Jewish blessing

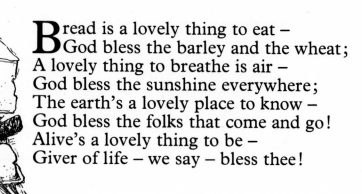

B read is a lovely thing to eat –
God bless the barley and the wheat;
A lovely thing to breathe is air –
God bless the sunshine everywhere;
The earth's a lovely place to know –
God bless the folks that come and go!
Alive's a lovely thing to be –
Giver of life – we say – bless thee!

All good gifts around us
Are sent from heaven above;
Then thank the Lord, O thank the Lord,
For all his love.

German hymn by Matthias Claudius (1740-1815)

Thank you, our heavenly Father, for harvest time:
for ripe fruit in the orchards
and berries in the hedges:
for the vegetable harvest and all food gathered in
and stored for winter days.

Sunday

This is the day which the Lord has made;
let us rejoice and be glad in it.
From Psalm 118

O God and Father of us all
help us to feel the joy of sharing
in the worship and praise of people in other countries.
May the children who sing the same praises as ours
know that we join with them in praising
and in showing our love for you as they do.

F or this new Sunday with its light,
For rest and shelter of the night,
We thank you, heavenly Father.
Through this new week but just begun,
Be near, and help us every one
To please you, heavenly Father.

T hank you, Lord, for the Christian church,
its work and witness in all ages and throughout
the world. Thank you for the church I attend,
and for the people who have taught me about you.
Help me to work for you as a member of the church.

O Almighty God,
we thank you for this special day
which you have given us for worship and rest.
Help us to keep it holy,
as the best day in all the week.
Teach everyone to love and honour your day,
that we may all rejoice and be glad in it.

S even whole days, not one in seven,
I will praise thee;
In my heart, though not in heaven,
I can raise thee.

George Herbert (1593-1632)

81

Birthdays

This is the word of the Lord, 'I have called you by name
and you are my own.'
From Isaiah 43

O loving God, today is my birthday.
For your care from the day I was born until today
and for your love, I thank you.
Help me to be strong and healthy,
and to show love for others, as Jesus did.

Prayer from Japan

T hou who hast given so much to me
Give one thing more, a grateful heart.

George Herbert (1593-1632)

Lord, we thank you for this and every happy birthday;
as we grow in age and strength
may we grow also in the knowledge of your love
and become more like you.

Lord Jesus, please help us to remember that you think
it is better to give things than to get them.
Please teach us to be givers, giving our time to help
at home, giving turns to each other at play,
and giving our best work at school.

My Father, all last year you took care of me and now
you have given me a birthday. I thank you for all
your goodness and kindness to me. You have given me loving
parents, a home, gifts and clothes. Thank you, God.
Help me to be a better child in my new year, to grow
strong, to study well, to work happily.

Prayer from India

Graces

Jesus took the bread, gave thanks to God and distributed
it to the people.
From John 6

Each time we eat,
may we remember God's love.

Prayer from China

Bless, dear Lord, my daily food.
Make me strong and make me good.

Come, dear Lord Jesus, be our guest,
And bless what thou hast given us.

German grace

Thank you, Father, for this food,
Which you gave to do us good.
Help us to remember you
All day long, in all we do.

84

We thank thee, Father, for thy care
For all thy children everywhere.
As thou dost feed us all our days
May all our lives be filled with praise.

Be present at our table, Lord;
Be here and everywhere adored.
Thy creatures bless, and grant that we
May feast in paradise with thee.

John Wesley (1703-1791)

For every cup and plateful,
God make us truly grateful.

Bless me, O Lord, and let my food
strengthen me to serve thee, for Jesus Christ's sake.

The New England Primer

Some ha'e meat, and canna eat,
And some wad eat that want it;
But we ha'e meat, and we can eat,
And sae the Lord be thankit.

Robert Burns (1759-1796)

Prayers for God's Blessing

Jesus took them in his arms and blessed them,
laying his hands upon them.
From Mark 10

God be merciful to us and bless us: and give us grace
to know his will and strength to do it.

The Lord bless us and keep us;
the Lord make his face shine upon us
and be gracious unto us:
the Lord lift up his countenance upon us,
and give us peace.

From Numbers 6

Be near me, Lord Jesus, I ask thee to stay
Close by me for ever, and love me, I pray.
Bless all the dear children in thy tender care;
And fit us for heaven to live with thee there.

Martin Luther (1483-1546)

God the Father, bless us;
God the Son, defend us;
God the Spirit, keep us
Now and evermore.

The grace of the Lord Jesus Christ
and the love of God
and the fellowship of the Holy Spirit
be with you all.

From 2 Corinthians 13

Prayers of Jesus

We ought always to pray and not lose heart.
From Luke 18

Our Father, which art in heaven,
hallowed be thy name.
Thy kingdom come.
Thy will be done in earth,
as it is in heaven.
Give us this day our daily bread.
And forgive us our trespasses,
as we forgive them
that trespass against us.
And lead us not into temptation,
but deliver us from evil:
For thine is the kingdom,
the power and the glory,
for ever and ever.

Father,
May your name be kept holy,
May your Kingdom come.
Give us day by day the food we need.
Forgive us our sins,
For we forgive everyone who has done us wrong.
And do not bring us to hard testing.

From Luke 11

I thank you, Father, that you listen to me.
I know that you always listen to me.

From John 11

I pray for . . . the men you gave me. O holy Father!
Keep them safe by the power of your name,
the name you gave me, so they may be one
just as you and I are one.

Jesus' prayer for his disciples, from John 17

Now my heart is troubled – and what shall I say?
Shall I say, 'Father, do not let this hour come upon me'?
But that is why I came, to go through this hour
of suffering. O Father, bring glory to your name!

From John 12

Forgive them, Father!
They don't know what they are doing.

Jesus' prayer from the cross, from Luke 23

Subject Index

This list supplements, and is designed to be used in conjunction with, the main contents list. Figures in bold type indicate a main theme as distinct from individual prayers.

Animals and pets 16–17

Bible 66–67

Birthdays 82–83

Blessing, of God 86–87
Bless all those I shall meet 43
God bless all those that I love 28
God of all our cities 10
Visit, we beseech thee 11

Books
Dear God, thank you for books 46

Christmas 72–73

Church
Thank you, Lord, for the Christian church 81

Creation 12
Thank you for the world so sweet 63

Death
Dear Lord Jesus, our little dog has died 17
Dear Lord Jesus, you cried 20
Jesus, our Lord, we praise you 74

Doctors and nurses
Great Father in heaven, thank you for doctors 41

Easter 74–75

Elderly
Lord Jesus, we remember today the old people 55

Evening and night 68–70

Family 28–29

Fear 30–31
The Lord is my shepherd 21

Forgiveness 14–15
Forgive them, Father 89
Lord Jesus, we remember how you forgave 15
We thank you, loving God 35

Friends 34–35

Games
Loving Father, on this day 47

Giving
Help us, Lord, to be thankful 51
Lord Jesus, please help us to remember 81

Graces 84–85

Handicapped
Lord Jesus, who for our sakes 41
Tend thy sick ones, O Lord Christ 41
Thank you, God, for my eyes 48

Harvest 78–79

Holidays 38–39

Homes 10–11

Hope
O God, who hast folded back the mantle 48

Illness 40–41

Leisure 46–47

Light 48–49

Listening to God
Lord, here is my Bible 67
O make my heart so still 33
We thank you for the beautiful snow 44
When I pray, I speak to God 32

Lord's Prayer
Our Father, which art in heaven 88
Father, may your name be kept holy 89

Love of God
Dear Father God, thank you for loving 62
Father in heaven, we praise you 50
May the love of God 11

Loving others 50–51
Holy Spirit, hear us 76
Lord Jesus, show us something to do 37

Mission(ary)
O God, who made the world 55
Thank you, Lord, for those who gave 66

Morning 8–9

Music
Thank you, God, for the gift of music 47

Obedience 18–19
May my mouth praise the love of God 8

Other countries 22–23
O God and Father of us all 81
O God, please comfort all the people 66

Parents
Bless, O Lord Jesus, my parents 29
Dear God our Father, we thank you 78
Dear Lord Jesus, please help us to do 19
Lord Jesus, I pray for those 20
Lord Jesus, we are glad 10
Thank you, O God our helper 37

Peace
God our Father, creator of the world 23
Lord, make me an instrument of thy peace 37
O God, make us children of quietness 32

Pentecost 76–77

People in need 54–55
Dear Father, please take special care 29
Lord Jesus, be with those 39
Lord Jesus, I pray for those 20
Lord Jesus, who for our sakes 41

Pleasing God 18–19
Father, we thank you for the night 8
Lord Jesus, show us something to do for you 37
Now another day is breaking 9

Praise 57, 26–27.
Let us with a gladsome mind 26
We thank thee, Father, for thy care 85

Presence of God
God be in my head 33
O God, my guardian 68
Space counts for nothing, Lord, with thee 22
The Lord is my shepherd 21
When I wake up in the morning 25

Protection of God 25, 30–31
Alone with none but thee, my God 43
Dear Father, hear and bless 17
Dear Father of the world family 22
Jesus, tender Shepherd, hear me 70
Lord, keep us safe this night 68
Lord, on the way to goodness 19
Visit, we beseech thee, O Lord 11

Race relations
Father of all men, we pray 58
God our Father, creator of the world 23

Rain 60–61

Refugees
Dear Jesus, you were taken as a baby refugee 55
O Lord, help us who roam 23

Road safety
God of all the steamships 43
Loving heavenly Father, who takes care of us all 43

School 58–59
Thank you, God, for this new day 27

Index of First Phrases

Sea
Dear God, be good to me 61
Dear Lord Jesus, who did not fear the sea 61
Thank you, God our heavenly Father, for holiday joys 38

Serving God 18–19
Dear Jesus, bless my hands today 53
Lord Jesus, take me this day 32
Lord, make me an instrument of thy peace 37
Teach us, good Lord, to serve thee 32

Statesmen
Please guide the leaders 22

Storms
Dear Lord Jesus, who did not fear the sea 61

Summer 44–45
Praise to God for summer days 38

Sunday 80–81

Teachers
Dear Lord Jesus, please help us to do 19
Thank you, God, for all our teachers 59
Thank you, O God our helper 37

Temptation
Lord, on the way to goodness 19

Thankfulness 62–63, 26–27, 78–79
Loving Father, we praise you 12
Thank you, God, for the day time 9

Thanksgiving 78–79

Toys
Dear God, thank you for our toys 46

Travel 42–43

Trinity
God the Father bless us 86
May the love of God 11
Praise God, from whom all blessings flow 26
The grace of the Lord Jesus Christ 86

Trouble 20–21

Unemployed
Please bless those who have no work 64

Vacation 38–39

Whitsun 76–77

Wind 60–61

Winter 44–45

Work 52–53, 64–65
Great Father in heaven, thank you for doctors and nurses 41

All by myself with the door shut 30
All good gifts around us 79
All things bright and beautiful 16
Alone with none but thee, my God 43

Be my guide, O Lord, I pray 53
Be near me, Lord Jesus, I ask thee to stay 86
Be present at our table, Lord 85
Blessed art thou, O Lord our God 78
Blessed Lord, who hast caused all 67
Bless all those that I shall meet 43
Bless, dear Lord, my daily food 84
Bless me, O Lord, and let my food 85
Bless, O Lord Jesus, my parents 29
Bread is a lovely thing to eat 78

Come, dear Lord Jesus, be our guest 84
Comfort, O Lord, we beseech thee 21

Day by day, dear Lord 19
Dear baby Jesus we have come 73
Dear Father God, thank you for loving 62
Dear Father God we thank you that we are able to see 54
Dear Father God, who made the world 45
Dear Father, hear and bless 17
Dear Father of the world family 22
Dear Father of us all we thank you 27
Dear Father, please take special care 29
Dear God be good to me 61
Dear God our Father, we thank you for all your care 78
Dear God, please look after everybody 64
Dear God, thank you for our books 46
Dear God, thank you for our holidays 38
Dear God, thank you for our toys 46
Dear God, we enjoy watching 47
Dear God, we pray for the workers of the world 65
Dear God who made the world 44
Dear God you are so very wonderful 57
Dear Holy Spirit, you are the one 77
Dear Jesus bless my hands today 53
Dear Jesus, you were taken as a baby 55
Dear Lord Jesus, help us to enjoy 53
Dear Lord Jesus I am thankful 34
Dear Lord Jesus, our little dog has died 17
Dear Lord Jesus, please help us to do 19
Dear Lord Jesus, we shall have this day 8
Dear Lord Jesus who did not fear 61
Dear Lord Jesus, you cried 20

Each time we eat, may we remember 84
Eternal God, the light of the minds 51

Father in heaven we praise you 50
Father, may your name be kept holy 89
Father of all men, we pray for boys and girls 58
Father of us all, thank you for another 58
Father, we thank you for animals 17
Father, we thank you for the night 8
Father, we thank you for the Scriptures 66
Forgive me, Lord, for thy dear Son 15
For every cup and plateful 85
Forgive them, Father! 89
For sausages, baked beans and crisps 62
For this new Sunday with its light 81

Give me, Lord, each day, time 46
God be in my head 33
God be merciful to us and bless us 86
God bless all the aunties 29
God bless all those that I love 28
God of all our cities 10
God of all the steamships 43
God of the coalmine 65
God our Father, creator of the world 23
God, our loving Father, thank you 57
God the Father bless us 86
God, this is your world 12
God who made the grass 25
Good Friday is a time of sadness 74
Goodnight! Goodnight! 68
Grant, heavenly Father, that as we keep 73
Great Father in heaven, thank you 41

Heavenly Father, as people turn to sleep 70
Heavenly Father, bless those who starve 55
Heavenly Father, thank you for the beauty 12
Heavenly Father, thank you for the joys of winter 44
Help us, Lord, to be thankful 51
Help us to keep the promises 18
Holy God, I'm happy 62
Holy God, who madest me 57
Holy Spirit, hear us 76

I bind unto myself today 25
I can say it to my family 8
I pray for the men you gave me 89
I thank you, Father 89
It's your world, God 12

Jesus Christ, thou child so wise 73
Jesus, friend of little children 34
Jesus, our Lord we praise you 74
Jesus, tender Shepherd, hear me 70
Jesus, when I am afraid 30
Jesus, when you were on earth 35
Jesus who died for me 74
Jesus, you're alive! 74

Let us with a gladsome mind 26
Lord, here is my Bible 67
Lord, how glad we are 25
Lord Jesus, be with those 39
Lord Jesus Christ we confess to you now 15
Lord Jesus, I am ill 40
Lord Jesus, I'm scared 30
Lord Jesus, I pray for those who will be unhappy 20
Lord Jesus, please help us to remember 83
Lord Jesus, show us something to do 37
Lord Jesus, take me this day 32
Lord Jesus we are glad that you lived 10
Lord Jesus, we remember how you forgave 15
Lord Jesus, we remember today 55
Lord Jesus, who for our sakes 41
Lord Jesus, you know that we are sad 21
Lord Jesus, you want us all 34
Lord keep us safe this night 68
Lord make me an instrument of thy peace 37
Lord of the loving heart 51
Lord, on the way to goodness 19
Lord, through this day 18
Lord, thy glory fills the heaven 57
Lord, we thank you for this 83
Love and praise to you we give 50
Loving Father, on this day 47
Loving Father, we praise you 12
Loving heavenly Father, who takes care 43

May my mouth praise the love of God 8
May the Lord Jesus Christ, who is the splendour 48
May the love of God our Father 11
My Father, all last year 83
My heart is overflowing 26

Now another day is breaking 9
Now my heart is troubled 89
Now the busy day is done 70

O Almighty God 81
O Father of goodness we thank you 27
O God and Father of us all 81
O God, forasmuch as without thee 77
O God, help us to remember the people 64
O God, look on us 27
O God, make us children of quietness 32
O God, my guardian, stay always with me 68
O God our heavenly Father, we are so very glad 59
O God, please comfort all the people 66
O God, the Father of all families 29
O God, we cannot do your will 76
O God, who hast folded back the mantle 48

O God, who knowest us to be set 31
O God, who made the world 55
O God, you made us 14
O Lord, bless our school 58
O Lord, help us to put you first 50
O Lord, help us who roam about 23
O Lord Jesus Christ, who received the children 70
O Lord Jesus, we remember how you had lessons 58
O Lord Jesus, who for love of us 72
O Lord, open my eyes to see 32
O Lord our God, give us by thy Holy Spirit 77
O loving God, today is my birthday 82
O make my heart so still 33
Open my eyes 19
O thou great Chief 48
O thou who art Lord of the harvest 78
Our Father in heaven, please forgive 14
Our Father in heaven we praise you 60
Our Father, maker of this wonderful world 47
Our Father, thank you for our pets 16
Our Father, which art in heaven 88
O ye summer and winter 44

Please bless those who have no work 64
Please, God, look after all those 10
Please guide the leaders 22
Praised be our Lord for the wind 61
Praise God from whom all blessings flow 26
Praise him, sun and moon 48
Praise to God for summer days 38
Put love into our hearts, Lord Jesus 50

Seven whole days, not one in seven 81
Some ha'e meat and canna eat 85
Space counts for nothing, Lord, with thee 22

Teach me, my God and king 53
Teach us, good Lord, to serve thee 32
Tend thy sick ones, O Lord Christ 41
Thank God for rain 61
Thank you, Father, for this food 85
Thank you for each happy day 27
Thank you for the beasts so tall 16
Thank you for the joy that comes 52
Thank you for the world so sweet 63
Thank you, God, for all good people 37
Thank you, God, for all our teachers 59
Thank you, God, for friends 35
Thank you, God, for holidays 39
Thank you, God, for my eyes 48
Thank you, God, for rain 60
Thank you, God, for the day-time 9
Thank you, God, for the fun of travelling 42
Thank you, God, for the gift of music 47
Thank you, God, for the joys of Christmas 72
Thank you, God, for this new day 27

Thank you, God, for this sunny morning 62
Thank you, God our heavenly Father, for holiday joys 38
Thank you, heavenly Father, for the wind 60
Thank you, Lord, for grannies and grandads 28
Thank you, Lord, for the Christian church 81
Thank you, Lord, for those who gave their lives 66
Thank you, O God our helper 37
Thank you, our heavenly Father, for harvest 79
The grace of the Lord Jesus Christ 86
The Lord bless us and keep us 86
The King of love my shepherd is 30
The Lord is my shepherd 21
The things, good Lord, that we pray for 52
Thou who hast given so much to me 82
Two little eyes to look to God 37

Visit, we beseech thee, O Lord 11

We thank thee, Father, for thy care 85
We thank thee, our heavenly Father 68
We thank you for the beautiful snow 44
We thank you, God, that everyone 28
We thank you, God, that you will be 38
We thank you, heavenly Father, that when Jesus 76
We thank you, loving God, that when we come 35
We thank you, O loving Father, for the joys 45
When I know how much you love me 30
When I pray I speak to God 32
When I wake up in the morning 25
Wind and ice and shrouding snow 44

You're marvellous, God 40

Acknowledgements

We would like to thank all those who have given us permission to include their prayers in this book, as indicated on the list below:

Mrs C. F. Alexander: p. 16(a).

Baker Book House: p. 25(d), from *God is No Stranger*, Sandra L. Burdick.

Mary K. Batchelor: pp. 17(b), 19(b), 20(b), 21(b), 28(c), 29(a), 66(b).

Blandford Press Ltd: pp. 18(a), 22(c), 27(c), 27(d), 29(b), 37(a), 37(d), 38(d), 39(b), 45(a), 47(a), 52(a), 61(a), 62(a), 62(d), 65(b), 70(a), 78(b), 85(f), from *The Infant Teacher's Prayer Book;* 50(d), from *The Junior Teacher's Prayer Book;* 68(b), from *The Senior Teacher's Prayer Book*, all edited by D. M. Prescott.

Church Information Office: H. Widdows, p. 16(c), Canon Dobson, p. 81(d), from *In Excelsis;* pp. 8(a), 12(d), 30(b), 30(d), 40(b), 62(c), 74(b), from *Prayabout*.

Church Missionary Society: pp. 39(a), 44(b), 51(b), 72(a), from *All Our Days*, edited by Irene Taylor and Phyllis Garlick.

Church Pastoral-Aid Society: Beryl Bye, p. 22(b), from *Please God;* Dick Williams, pp. 14(a), 67(a), Christopher Idle, p. 15(a), from *Prayers for Today's Church*.

Concordia Publishing House Ltd: p. 34(b), from *Dear Father in Heaven*, compiled by Robert H. Schlesselmann and Luella Spitzack Ahrens; p. 86(d), from *Little Folded Hands*.

Curtis Brown Ltd: pp. 8(b), 23(b), 82(a), 83(c), 84(a), from *Children's Prayers from Other Lands*.

Duckworth and Co. Ltd: p. 61(d), from *Thanksgiving for the Earth*.

Estate of Ogden Nash: Ogden Nash p. 9(a), from *Parents Keep Out*.

Evans Bros Ltd: A. W. L. Chitty, p. 78(d), from *Child Education*.

Hodder and Stoughton Ltd: pp. 30(c), 35(b), 46(c), 48(e), 81(c), from *A Patchwork Prayer Book*, Janet Lynch-Watson; Hope Freeman, p. 12(a), Nina Hinchy, p. 17(a), Nancy Martin,

p. 61(b), Graham Salmon, p. 64(c), from *Prayers for Children and Young People*, compiled by Nancy Martin; p. 72(b), from *Prayers for the Home;* pp. 10(b), 14(a), 15(b), 16(b), 41(b), 50(b), 58(b), 58(d), 60(a), 64(b), from *Prayers for Younger Children*, Brenda Holloway; pp. 38(a), 46(a), 46(b), 47(b), 55(b), 70(b), 76(b), from *Well God, Here We Are Again . . .*, John Bryant and David Winter.

Ladybird Books Ltd: pp. 38(b), 60(b), 60(c), 79(b), from *The Ladybird Book of Prayers Through the Year*, compiled by Hilda I. Rostron.

Longman Group Ltd: pp. 27(b), 85(c), from *An Anthology of Prayers*, A. S. T. Fisher.

Lutterworth Press: p. 44(d), from *Children's Prayers and Praises*, Ella Forsyth Wright; p. 53(c), from *A Book of Prayers for Boys and Girls*, Elfreyda Wightman.

Mowbray and Co. Ltd: pp. 10(a), 43(c), 65(a), from *God of All Things*, Joan Gale Thomas; pp. 48(d), 51(c), 73(b), 77(b), 83(a), from *The Lord is my Shepherd*; pp. 43(d), 50(c), from *Talking to God*, Ena V. Martin.

Frederick Muller Ltd: pp. 17(c), 85(b), from *Hymns and Prayers for Children*.

National Christian Education Council: pp. 22(a), 81(a), from *Missionary Prayers and Praises*, Hilda I. Rostron.

The National Society for Promoting Religious Education: p. 32(c), from *Worship in Junior Schools;* Mrs. E. Rutter Leatham, p. 63(a), from *Hymns and Songs for Children;* p. 74(c), from *Thy Kingdom Come;* R. R. Brookes, p. 32(d), from *Unto the Hills*.

Oxford University Press: pp. 11(a), 25(b) altd., 43(a), 55(a), 57(a), 59(a), 59(b), 73(c), from *Infant Prayer*, Margaret Kitson; pp. 10(c), 51(a), 55(c), 58(c), 64(a), 74(c), 76(c), from *Time and Again Prayers*, compiled by Janet Cookson and Margaret Rogers; pp. 12(b), 32(a), 41(a), 48(a), 58(a), 68(d), 73(a), from *Prayers and Hymns for Junior Schools;* W. J. Mathams, p. 34(a).

Pitman Publishing Ltd: p. 45(b), from *Starting the Day*, J. T. Hilton.

The Saint Andrew Press: p. 47(c), from *Sunday, Monday . . .*, R. S. Macnicol.

Schofield and Sims Ltd: 27(e).

Scripture Union: p. 37(e), from *C.S.S.M. Chorus Book no. 1;* p. 12(c), from *Family Prayers* (1971); pp. 18(b), 66(a), from *Family Prayers* (1974); pp. 9(b), 20(a), 30(a), 38(c), 66(c), 74(d), 83(b), from *Let's Talk to God*, Zinnia Bryan; pp. 35(c), 40(a), 42(a), 55(d), 57(d), 77(a), from *Let's Talk to God Again*, Zinnia Bryan; 44(a), from *Prayers*, Stephen Winward and Godfrey Robinson.

SPCK: p. 84(b), from *Baby's First Prayers*, Mrs A. C. Osborn Hann; pp. 37(c), 76(a), 78(a), 81(b), 85(a), from *A Brownie Guide Prayer Book*, compiled by Rosalie Wakefield.

Donald Soper, p. 47(d).

Henry Z. Walck Inc.: pp. 29(d), 68(a), 84(c), 85(d), from *First Prayers*.

H. E. Walter Ltd: p. 29(c), from *Little Prayers for Little People*, Kathleen Partridge.

Special thanks for help in the early stages to Mr A. Barker, SPCK archivist; Miss Christine Aspinall of the Methodist Missionary Society; and the Rev. Dick Fry, formerly with the Wycliffe Bible Translators.

Every effort has been made to trace and contact copyright owners. If there are any inadvertent omissions in the acknowledgements we apologize to those concerned.

93